500 GREAT Heartwarming Expressions

For Scrapbooking & Cards

by Sandy Redburn
Artwork by Suzanne Carillo

Crafty Secrets Publications
15430 78A Ave.
Surrey, B.C. Canada
V3S 8R4

ISBN 0-9686648-1-4

Table of Contents - Book 4

Themes and Creative Idea Pages

Introduction

It's no surprise that scrapbooking has become such a popular hobby. It offers people of all skill levels the chance to be creative while accomplishing an important task - saving memories. The trend in preserving memories has produced some wonderful effects. What else could offer a more positive lasting way to build a person's sense of self worth, security and feelings of being loved than to have specials pages created that celebrate their life and accomplishments? When you have a hobby powerful enough to strengthen family ties and bond friendships, it's easy to see how it can spill over into many areas within the craft industry.

With the ever growing and fantastic range of great supplies and products available today, you can now create all kinds of personalized memory keepsakes. This book will inspire you with creative ideas and versatile ways you can create treasured scrapbook pages, cards and memory keepsakes that help convey your "message" with heart appealing personality!

The People Behind These Pages

The Author

I'm **Sandy Redburn**, the author and publisher of the Heartwarming Expressions Books. I'm the "idea lady" behind these books and it seems I've become addicted to dreaming up new expressions and showing people creative ways to use them. After completing the first Heartwarming Book in 1995, I never would have dreamed I would be doing book #4, but the ideas just keep coming! Now that I've become a certified scrap-a-holic I am especially proud of this book.

Sandy

The Artist

Suzanne Carillo is a multi-talented freelance artist and the main contributor for the artistic lettering and almost all of the illustrations including the cover artwork on this new fourth book. Her artistic talents are showcased throughout the book in every style, from adorable to stylish and heritage themes. The humor and whimsy she puts into her artwork is sure to make you smile as you look through these pages.

Other Contributors

Diane Pruss, owner of Splash Graphics, has done the graphic design and created all of the marketing materials for all four of the Heartwarming Expressions Books. Diane also lent her hand this time to lettering some of the expressions and wow, is she talented! Two of my favorites are "Backyard Boys with Their Toys" and "Two Hearts Shall Beat As One."

Cindy van Koll, is a talented and certified scrap-a-holic who played a big part in putting together the sample scrapbook pages and cards you will see photographed in this book. Cindy also got talked into creating some great pages including pages 30, 54, 66 and 91.

Diana Haines, a calligrapher for over twenty years, feels the art of lettering is a hobby worth practicing, as it provides a way to add your own hand lettered creativity to countless projects. Diana also teaches calligraphy and says many students feel it's great stress therapy. Diana has hand lettered over fifty wonderful expressions in this book.

Also, many thanks to Shelly Ehbrecht and Debi Carrington, for their wonderful contributions in hand lettering.

How To Make This Book Work

You Get to Decide

I think the secret to making this book work for you, is to remember that there are no rules written in stone. One good rule though, is to always use archival supplies and paper for any project you want to last for years. Depending on your projects, interests, skill level, budget and imagination you can put this book into action in countless ways.

Thanks to technology, we now have so many innovative and wonderful supplies, techniques and possible surfaces available to decorate. This book is primarily geared towards scrap-booking and card ideas, but I believe as you look through these pages, you will see many of the expressions can also work for creating and embellishing a variety of crafts and keepsakes.

In the following pages I will cover some of the basic techniques, tools and supplies commonly used. If you are new to any of these ideas I encourage you to dive into any that interest you and read more in-depth books, visit web sites, take classes and explore the full creative potential that each offers.

Why Expressions Work

This book is jam-packed with over 550 expressions, quips and quotes (I got carried away again). Some are sentimental, some mushy, inspirational, feel good, humorous and silly. I've tried to include a large variety of themes and create expressions to suit various occasions, family members and friends. Adding expressions to scrapbook pages, cards and keepsakes can create warmth, personality and convey a special message. Choose expressions that convey the feelings and sentiments you want to capture. Keep in mind, some expressions may work better if you alter the wording, or simply change singular words to

plural. When you find yourself coming up with your own expressions, there is a spot to add them on page 90.

Lettering Possibilities

Lettering in scrapbooks includes a large variety of creative possibilities. Some people prefer to do all their own hand lettering on their scrapbook pages using acid free pens and markers. Some stick on ready made alphabets, embossed letters, die cuts, computer fonts and so on. Others trace or photocopy expressions and page toppers, hand coloring the lettering to suit their pages. In the sample pages shown in this book we've used the last two methods but you can use the methods and supplies you like best. Anything you want to save for years should be traced or copied onto acid free paper.

Choosing Paper

With any scrapbook or card project, one of the most important supplies is paper. Papers come in every hue and in various weights and textures, in solid colors, patterns, embossed, glittered, metallic, mulberry, vellum, velvet and more. You can also create different effects with paper by folding, tearing, embossing, punching, stamping, coloring and so forth. When scrapbooking, it's best to lay your photos out to see what you would like to include in your page layout and what type of colors and style will best complement your photographs. There are so many shades in colors, it can be helpful to bring photos along when picking out paper to get the right match. Make some notes on possible page headings and expressions you want to use. You will then have an idea of how much paper you need for lettering and matting.

Hand Lettering Tips and Tricks

Some Simple Rules

You can trace or photocopy the expressions and designs in this book, which I will discuss on the following page. You may also see some expressions, or have words you want to use, which you want to hand letter yourself. Your own hand lettering can add extra personality to your pages. Here are a few helpful tools and tips. You will need a soft lead pencil, clear ruler, good art eraser and the pens or markers you want to use for your lettering. Decide on a suitable style without picking anything too difficult to begin with.

Pencil your lettering out first to get your spacing and size right. Practice on scrap paper, to test which pens and colors work best. Lettering doesn't have to be even, but try for consistency in spacing the letters and words. Rather than letter right onto your page or card, you may want to do your lettering on different paper or cardstock. Once it's inked, it can be trimmed and double matted for a nice touch. When inking lettering, hold the pen upright and pull it towards you rather than pushing it away for better pen control. Don't press hard and rotate your pen to keep the tip in good shape. Erase any pencil lines.

Lettering Personality

You can add emotion and personality to lettering by the style you choose and the embellishments you add. As you can see in the samples below, although they are only words, each one conveys a feeling associated with the word. This book is filled with all kinds of lettering styles to inspire you. All you have to do is get creative!

Adding Color

Who wouldn't love the vast array of colored pens and markers available in every tip size, style and ink to produce different effects. Look at the colored samples here, displayed in stores and in magazines for inspiration. You can trace or copy chunky lettering onto colored paper. You can use embossing pens over lettering with colored embossing powders. I also love watercolor pencils & chalks for adding artistic flair to lettering.

Creative Possibilities

Tracing Tips & Tricks

You can use this book just for ideas and freehand the expressions and graphics, you can photocopy them, or trace them. Tracing is popular for a number of reasons. Tracing gives you the freedom to trace only what you want to use, deleting or adding words, parts of designs, or changing an oval inside a frame to a rectangle and so on. You can use a bright window or light box to trace, using a pencil. Some light boxes have higher wattage bulbs, allowing you to trace on cardstock.

Photocopying

With the purchase of this book you can use the expressions and designs as clip art and photo-copy them for your own personal use. Have the designs you want enlarged or reduced on a good quality copier. To prevent any show through from the other side of the page, you can place a black piece of paper on top of the page being copied. From your copy, cut out what you need and lay it out on plain white paper, and glue with adhesive. I love Zig 2 Way Glue Pens because they allow you to remove and reposition every-thing. *I used them to glue every expression on these pages when putting this book together!* Photocopy your layout page onto your final good paper or cardstock.

Most color photocopiers can also turn black ink into another color. I had the large heritage frame and expression shown on page 52 copied in medium brown. My mom's wedding photo was color tinted back in the 50's. My favorite way to achieve this same effect is to use Decorating Chalks on black and white photocopies.

Using Your Computer

Some people feel anything printed off a computer loses any handcrafted appeal, but computers can open doors to all sorts of creative possibilities. Many people simply don't like their own handwriting, or have a hard time staying neat and prefer to do their journaling using a computer font. There is an endless array of type styles available. In fact, a company called Inspire Graphics from Pleasant Grove, Utah can create your own hand lettering in a font for you. You can use your different styles of computer fonts to print out these expressions. This will enable you to quickly turn any expression into a page topper that matches your journaling font. If you still want the hand lettered look, you can print out the lettering to simply help you determine your outlay and spacing. Many computers come with creative software, or you can purchase CD's for lettering that will enable you to add color and all kinds of cool effects. *This book may be on a CD one day!*

Good quality color ink jet printers and scanners have come down in price and also offer great benefits. There are all kinds of innovative products for printing on, like acid free papers, sheets of fabric, magnetic and sticker papers. Some of the new printers will even accept 12" x 12" paper. With a scanner, you can scan in the pages from this book and change the size of any expressions and graphics. With a color printer and software you can even change the black ink to a different color. You can also scan in photos and with photo software you can re-size, crop, tint, manipulate and also e-mail album pages.

Creating Special Cards

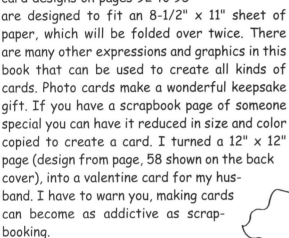

Hand made cards can be a treasured gift all by themselves. The ready-to-copy card designs on pages 92 to 95 are designed to fit an 8-1/2" x 11" sheet of paper, which will be folded over twice. There are many other expressions and graphics in this book that can be used to create all kinds of cards. Photo cards make a wonderful keepsake gift. If you have a scrapbook page of someone special you can have it reduced in size and color copied to create a card. I turned a 12" x 12" page (design from page, 58 shown on the back cover), into a valentine card for my husband. I have to warn you, making cards can become as addictive as scrapbooking.

Making Unique Envelopes

Unique envelopes can make any greeting more fun and special. You will find an envelope template on page 96 with matching stamps for the four card designs. You can also open any size envelope and trace around it. It will be sturdier if it's copied onto card stock and then cut out. To make an envelope, lay the template on an 8-1/2" x 11" sheet of paper, trace around the outside edge and cut out. Fold along dotted lines and glue corners #1 and #2. Apply adhesive around edge of #3 and glue down. You can make envelopes from patterned paper, your child's artwork, old maps, magazines, calendars, comics and other imaginative sources. If mailing, make sure the name and address can be clearly read by the post office, using a plain label if necessary. Color the stamp design and glue on, leaving space for real postage. Insert your card and seal the envelope with a sticker.

Other Creative Ideas

There are tools and supplies that will allow you to add expressions to just about any surface you can dream up. For example, if you were throwing an "over the hill party" for someone, you could put an expression on an invitation, card, keepsake gift, wrapping paper, party hat, plastic tablecloth, balloons, banner and more. You could then take lots of pictures and scrapbook the big event.

You can also take any small photo, add a frame and expression and turn it into a magnet or bookmark and have it laminated. I've even had favorite mini pages reduced to magnet size on a color copier. I then covered both sides with clear adhesive I found by the roll at Wal-Mart and added magnetic tape.

You can also use the expressions and graphics to create announcements, calendars, book covers, keepsake boxes, seasonal and kids craft projects. The empty frames on pages 97-99 are perfect for your journaling or for creating personal gift tags.

There are so many fun and easy things for all skill levels that can be made, it would be impossible to list them all here (hey, this could be a new book). It's easy to get hooked (guilty party here) and if this sounds interesting, check out my list of 99 Places To Put An Expression, included on the inside cover of the first three Heartwarming Expressions books. You can also visit www.craftysecrets.com for ideas and projects using expressions. Remember to feed your creativity regularly and most of all, have fun!

A moment lasts but a second. The memory can last f·o·r·e·v·e·r.

Hello World - I'm Here!

Special Delivery

Once upon a time

in a land called

a truly special baby named

was born and the world became a nicer place.

BABY LOVE

Sneak Preview

WOW
we're pregnant!

FROM THE MOMENT THEY PLACED YOU IN MY ARMS YOU SNUGGLED RIGHT INTO MY HEART

Congratulations!
We just knew you had it in you.

bee-bop baby

Peek-A-Boo
We see you!

Make Room For BABY

YOU WERE WORTH EVERY
C·O·N·T·R·A·C·T·I·O·N

BROADWAY BABY

Life was so Boring Before YOU

BALD IS BEAUTIFUL

THERE'S A NEW KID IN TOWN

These Feet Were Made For Eating

9

We Made a Wish and You Came True

The First Time We Ever Saw Your Face We Fell in Love

Our Shining Star

Welcome Sweet Baby

We've Been Waiting for You

"We've Added A New Member To Our Family Tree"

BABY

welcome to our WORLD

OH BABY You're BEAUTIFUL!

Cute as a Bug

Little Bug A Boo we Love you!

Here she is all peaches and cream, our sweet little girl, our long awaited dream

Oh Joy Oh Joy We have a Boy!

DROOL IS COOL

GOT MILK?

I'M TOO SEXY FOR MY DIAPER

TIME 4 BONDING

Teething Is A Real PAIN!

NEW ROOKIE on the BLOCK

egg
Hunting
Madness!

EASTER OUTFITS
~ ON PARADE ~

EGG-TREME
FUN!

All SHINED Up
With Somewhere to Go

Read All About Us!

BRAVO BRAVO

Diploma Dazzeler

BIG Birthday Bash

HATS Off To You GRADUATE!

Prom Night Delight

Hip-Hip Hooray
It's My Birthday Today!

DANCING The Night Away

THE BIG BIG DAY
We're Celebrating YOU!

BIRTHDAYS Are a Piece of Cake

The Razzel Dazzel Smile Of No More Braces

Food oh Glorious FOOD!

Christmas
the Season of Heart

For Christmas Give Your Heart

✳ ✳ Snowflakes fall ✳ ✳
when the angels have a pillow fight

♫ Here we come a-caroling
A-CAROLING WE COME

🌿 Holly-Days 🌿
Are Here Again

Christ
is the
Heart &
Soul of
Christmas

Gathered round the Christmas Tree   with shining faces full of glee

Feeling More Stuffed than the Stockings

CHRISTMAS JOY
To Every Little
Girl & Boy

Our Little Christmas Angels

Don't be naughty because here's the scoop All you will get is Some reindeer poop!

Glad Tidings of Joy

Reindeer Lane
Rooftop Parking

To the Spirit of
Christmases
yet to come

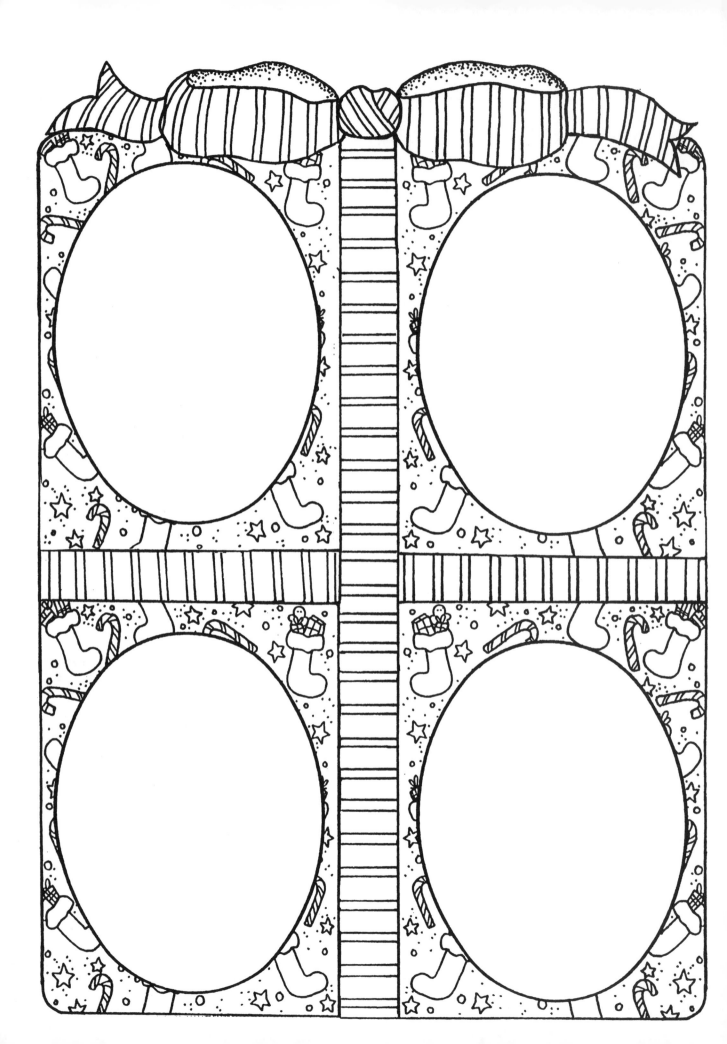

A Magical Mistletoe Moment

A Couple of Christmas Cuties

No Sneaking or Peeking Till Christmas Day!

Snowman's Prayer: Please Freeze Amen

The best Christmas gift of all OUR FAMILY All happily wrapped up in one another

Dear Santa Leave Presents Take ~~Brother~~ Sister

The Best Gift Of All... Is Each Other

*Dashing*through*the*snow*

It's BABES IN TOYLAND

The Perfect Man - A Snowman
He's a Well rounded guy
He comes With his own Broom
He is Very Cool
If he Misbehaves - He's in hot water!

B Cool

Snowmen are the Coolest Guys

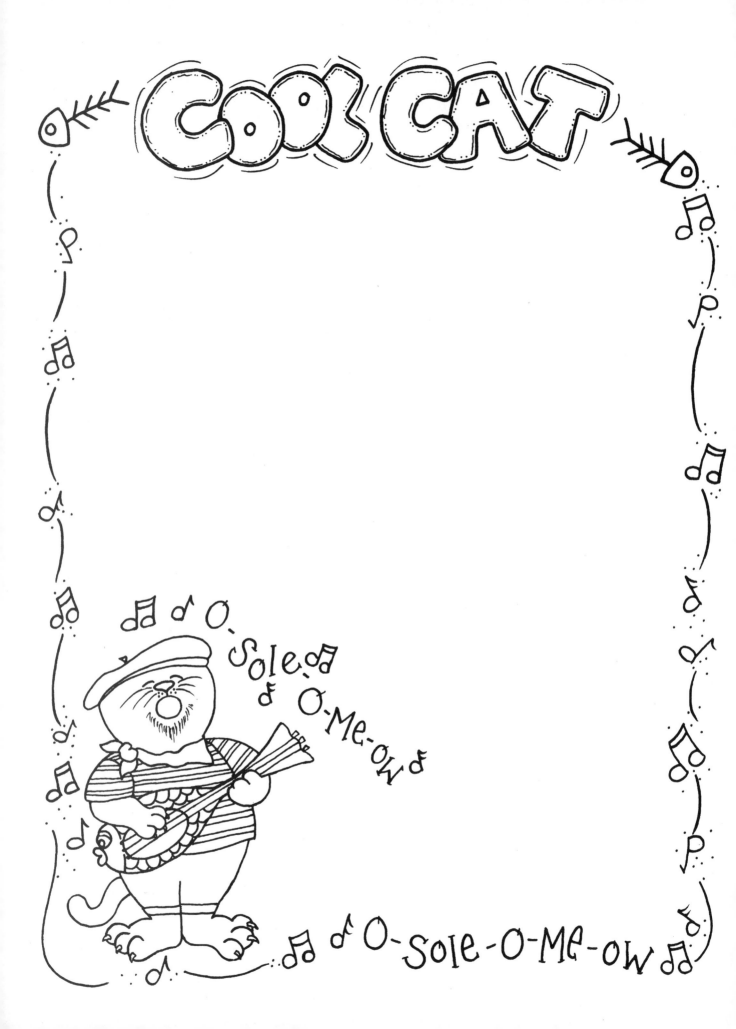

Pampered Puss

Feline Sublime

BRAT-CAT AWARD

Cat got your tongue?

LOVE ME... LOVE MY CAT

The Smallest Feline Is A Masterpiece
Leonardo Da Vinci

Into every life must fall

a little cat hair

FAT CAT

If purring is how cats smile, I have one HAPPY pussy cat.

WHAT A SNUGGLE-PUSS

CLEOCATRA

Purr-fect Pals

Cats aren't clean, They're just covered in CAT SPIT

—John Nichols

Feline Frisky Tung-Nite

19

I RUFF YOU

THE FAMILY MASCOT

TOP DOG

WELCOME TO THE DOG HOUSE

Super Dog Show Candidate

Wagging My Tail To Spoiled Rotten

Puppy Love

To ERR is Human To Forgive CANINE

Pampered Pooch

To Find Your Inner Child, Own A Puppy!

A DOG HAS A SOUL OF A PHILOSOPHER
-PLATO

DOG IS OK BEWARE OF WIFE

I do have one dog trick— I can wag my tail Backwards

a new leash on life.

21

I DON'T DO FETCH

CATS RULE DOGS DROOL

LOOK what the cat dragged in!

This is my OTHER CHILD DRESSED IN FUR

Dogs come to their owners Cats summon their staff

Dogs CHOW DOWN ON ANYTHING Cats ORDER off ROOM SERVICE

CATS MOTTO: THE DOG DID IT!

BAD to the BONE

EVERYONE needs a FURRY FRIEND

If its true we start looking like our pets, Help!

One cat leads to another, to another, to another

I love my Pets !

My Other Pets Are Dust Bunnies

Down on the farm is where the best memories grow

ALL COUNTRY BOY

Go West Young Man

Ride Em' Horsey!

Yippee-Yi-a!

Sweet Country Pickins'

PRESERVING THE PAST

FARMING IS the LiFe FoR Me

100% Purebred Country

Pure Country Gal

CASANOVA COWBOY

Little Cowpoke

25

Family Ties Are Bound By Love

Delightful
Dazzling
Darling
Daughter(s)
Dear

FAMILY is What Makes A Heart Feel At HOME

Super
Sensational
Special
Son!

Every SISTER Needs a BROTHER Like YOU!

Sisters are different flowers from the same garden

The journey of sharing both laughter and tears
SISTERHOOD
connected together through a lifetime of years

Little Mr. Son-shine

My Buddy ~ My Brother

Parents are the ones that always clap the loudest for You

Smart, Goodlooking, and as Sweet as Can Be It's no Surprise... It's Heredity

27

Family Matters

There is no other like my Marvelous Magnificent Mother

Daddy's Little Helper

VIVA MOTHERS!!

MOM stands for MOTHER not Made of Money

DYNAMITE DAD!

NOTHING IN LIFE CAN HOLD MORE JOYS OR MORE TEARS, CAN MAKE YOU MORE PROUD OR MORE TIRED, OR GIVE BACK MORE REWARDS THAN BEING A MOTHER

my Dad my Hero

Just me & my Dad

IT'S HOP ON POP TIME!

A Father is the Hands That Hold You Safe
— Jane Swan b. 1943

Like Father Like Son

THEY SAY THERE'S NO OTHER THAT CAN TAKE THE PLACE OF M·O·T·H·E·R
— GEORGE BERNARD SHAW

The world has no such flower in any land, and no such pearl in any sea, as any babe on any mother's knee.
ALGERMON CHARLES SWINBURNE

You can use the oval
or the rectangle for
this frame.

You Are Our Son-Shine

We Can't Help it... Good Looks Run in Our Family

My AUNTie is AWESOME

A-1 UNCle

LOOK WHO'S A Grandma NOW!

The PROUDEST Papa

Angels can't be everywhere so God created

GRANDMAS

The Nicest NaNa

Grandchildren are God's Reward For putting up with your Kids

GRANDKiDS are the best MEDICINE ♡ FoR A ♡ YOUNG HEART

WHO NEEDS SANTA when you have Nana & Papa

GRANDparents help make the World a GRANDER place

Gallery of Good Friends
Original Works of Heart

Priceless

One of A KIND

ORIGINAL

Rare

I count myself in nothing else so happy
as in a soul remembering good friends.

William Shakespeare

The Best Antiques
to Collect
Are Old Friends

Girlfriend it's True
Life Would be so Blue
Without You!

The ornaments
of a house are the
FRIENDS
who frequent it

Ralph Waldo Emerson

Friends like you
are like fine art,
so rare, so treasured,
just priceless with
heart!

A Friend
may well be
reckoned the
masterpiece
of nature
Ralph Waldo Emerson

You have a Heart
of gold

Dear Old Friend
Even though we
may be apart
You have a
permanent spot
reserved in my
heart

You are the happy face
that makes my world a nicer place

With friends Like These Life's A Breeze

Fabulously Fun Fine Friends

Fine
Friends

LOVE AND JOY
this message sends,
Because there's nothing nicer than
DEAR OLD FRIENDS

Two Teas In A Pod

Friendship is the flower that blossoms in the heart

your friendship surrounds me Like a warm Hug

FRIENDS ARE THE SUNSHINE OF LIFE

You & me BUDS forever

Friends

make the earth a Glorious Garden

DIAMONDS May Be Precious, But you Girlfriend Are Priceless!

EVERYTHING EVERYTHING is twice as nice when shared

A Crop of Great Friends

make for Great Memories

35

Pajama Party Pals

Little Darlings

Groovy Gals

Brainy & Beautiful

Ooooo La~La

OH, OH, This One Has More Spice Than Sugar

~What Style, What Grace, What a Silly Face!

There's a WILD Little Woman Somewhere in Each of Us

Spinny? Who's Spinny?

Drama Queen

What-Ever!!!

FORGET the Sugar & Spice GIRLS are made from Real♡HEART ~GUTS~ and Soul

Giggling Girlfriend Get-Togethers

Social Butterflies

Girl Talk

BOY CRAZY

DANCING QUEEN

LADIES IN VOGUE

Beauty Queen

If The Shoe Fits... I Want One In Every Color!

Perfectly Pretty in Pink

Stepping Out ON GIRLS NIGHT OUT

PRETTY WOMAN

Which Way To Hollywood?

No Self Respecting Girl Should be Without a Feather Boa
— Yves Saint Laurent

Dazzling Damzels Dressed Divinely

Fashion Show Fabulous

39

BOY MEETS WORLD

You're Out of This World!

MOMMY & DADDY'S FAVORITE ACTION HERO

Hello Mr Handsome!

BACKYARD BOYS

with their

100% BOY

Just Say NO To Girl Cooties

Boy, oh boy he's becoming a man

DASHING and DEBONAIR

VICTIM OF BEDHEAD

WAY Cool THAT'S YOU!

You the man!

Such a Charmer

SOME STYLING, HAPPENING, KIND OF GUYS

BOYS R US

Crazy 4 Cars

So Many Girls So Little Time

Radical DUDE

41

REAL MEN DO COOK
(we just say No to dish pan hands)

100% MACHO MAN

IT'S a GUY THING

MAN of THE HOUR

Me & My Girl

Certified STUD Muffin

Guys JUST WANNA HAVE FUN

KISS ME I'M YOUR PRINCE

Buddies + BEER = MALE Bonding MOMENT

Handsome Hunks

So, women are from Venus~ I always thought they were from another PLANET!
~Man from Mars

Tool TIME WITH MR. FIX-IT

Nice Set of Wheels

Christopher Columbus didn't need DIRECTIONS So neither do I.

A GHOULISH GROUP OF TREATERS

Hey Ghoul-Friend Your Outfit is **Spook**-tacular!

Who ever said Halloween was for kids didn't know US!

Wickedly Witchy WOMAN

Spook-tacularly Boo-tiful

Batty Over Boo!

Ghoulish Greetings Goblins

HAPPY HAUNTS TO YOU!

Free Spells & Hexes Here

Slimey-Gooey Pumpkin Brains

Sugar Bugs

Crazed By CANDY MADNESS!

SAC -O- CANDY

MUNCHIES 4 MONSTERS

Tasty LOOT

OUR Little Monsters

Little pumpkins all in a row putting on a Halloween show

45

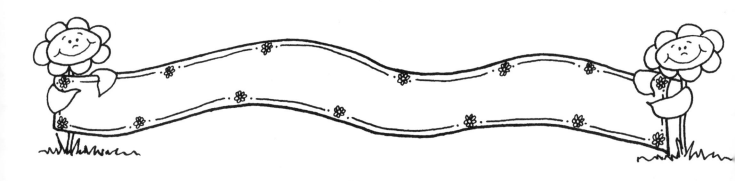

ONE IN A MILLION

I AM What I AM Because Of ME

Inspiration

Our Shining Star

Never Never Never Never Give Up
-Sir Winston Churchill

tall oaks
from·little·acorns·grow

Whatever you Are Be A Good ONE
-Abraham Lincoln

Write it on Your Heart That Every Day is the Best Day of the Year
Ralph Waldo Emerson

L'Chaim
Hebrew Toast "To Life"

Everything is Possible

You Miss 100% of the Shots You Never TAKE
-Wayne Gretzky

Cultivate Your Garden Within

We can't change fate, But we can change our view

READY TO TAKE ON THE WORLD!

See the Good in Life & You Will Feel It's Glory

47

Ideas & Supply List
for color sample pages 49 & 50

1. We Made a Wish ... *From pg. 10*
These adorable frames work together or by themselves for mini size pages or cards.
Divide your page onto four different pastel colors. Copy the design on white and color it to match the page with pastel pencils or chalks.

2. Cute As A Bug *From pg. 11*
These cute bugs and expressions also work great on a page.
Make the card by folding white embossed bug paper from Lasting Impressions in half. Copy design on white, color bugs with colored pencils and mat with purple. Inside, add another expression.

3. Family Matters *From pg. 32*
This fun page tells it like it is!
Copy the page on white, color with watercolor pencils and cut out. For background room idea, use solid green and Provo Craft gold and white dot paper. Also from Art Impressions green stripe and leaf paper. You can add the cat from page 22.

4. Families Bloom ... *From pg. 26*
A great page for family photos.
Copy page on white then color and cut out. Double mat flowers with green check pattern and solid gold from Keeping Memories Alive. Mount on daisy yellow from Keeping Memories Alive. Mat photos with brown, then to a strip of green and gold down the middle of page.

5. I Ruff You *From pg. 20*
Use any family mascot on this page and change the heading to suit photo.
Copy page on pink and yellow, cut the inside frame and page topper from yellow and the outside frame from pink. Mount on a glitter pink paper from Paper Adventures. Use felts and glitter to add pizzazz to frame.

6. My Dad My Hero *From pg. 29 & 40*
This mini page would make a great Father's Day card or gift when framed.
Copy the graphic and saying from page 29 and the frame from page 40 on white. Use felt pens for bright super hero colors. Shade frame with blue pencil crayon. Mount on cloud paper.

7. Messy Munchkins *From pg. 55.*
What mess is your munchkin into?
Copy design on ivory and tan. Cut and mount as shown with dark brown. Color munchkin graphic and mount on Provo Craft green grass paper.

14. Gallery of Good Friends *From pg. 32*
Create a gallery for friends from the past or friends today.
Copy page on pale pink, cut out frames and color with watercolor pencils. Color the page title, punch corners and mount on Cottage Collection burgundy from Keeping Memories Alive. Mount everything on burgundy velvet from Paper Adventures. To mount on 12x12" page add a strip of the cottage print on each side.

2. Sugar & Spice *From pg. 37*
Girl talk is full of fun sayings, strictly for girls.
Copy expressions on white and double mat with gray speckle and black paper. This combination works great for black and white photos.

3. Large Heritage Frame *From pg. 30*
Use this lovely frame to enhance a treasured photo.
For this heritage look, color copy the black frame and expression (pg.65) in brown ink on cream stock. Cut out the frame and expression and color with pastel chalks. Mat on soft green and mount both on Cottage Collection - Antique Cream Dark Foliage from Keeping Memories Alive.

4. Snapshots of Time *From pg. 64*
Capture any happy memory here.
Copy design on moss green and ivory and also on white paper (for a filmstrip template) Cut out centers in template and lay over photos. Number and mark each with grease pencil. Cut out photos. Cut filmstrip from green, cut film canister from ivory, glue together and mount on rust. Glue photos on. Double mat title in green and rust. Color the photo corners on ivory and cut out. Double mat photos with rust and green, add corners and mount on black.

5. Wedding Bells *From pg. 88.*
These frames will work with many other themes and page titles.
Copy page on white. Color frames with watercolor pencils and cut centers out. Mount photos from back and mount on purple velvet from Paper Adventures.

One Scrapbook Page Like One Cookie Is Never Enough!

1. We Made a Wish and You Came True
The First Time We Ever Saw Your Face We Fell in Love
Our Shining Star
Welcome Sweet Baby
We've Been Waiting for You

2. Little BugABoo We Love You!
Cute as a Bug

3. Family Matters
The Paton Family 1995
Bill Sheila Alana Brett & Shadow
DAD
MOM
Hey Sister!
Oh Brother

4. FAMILIES BLOOM with Love
Nik & Ike
LOVE

FAMILY IS What Makes A Heart Feel At HOME

Pg. 27

5. I RUFF YOU
THE FAMILY MASCOT

6. JUST ME & my DAD
my Dad my Hero

7. MESSY LITTLE MUNCHKIN
Hey a little dirt never hurt anyone

1. Gallery of Good Friends
Original Works of Heart

Priceless
One of A KIND
Margaret
Alice & Emma
ORIGINAL
Rare
Beatrice & Florence
Elizabeth & Margaret

2. FORGET the Sugar & Spice GIRLS are made from Real Heart ~ GUTS ~ and Soul

There's a WILD Little Woman Somewhere in Each of Us

Summer of 1960
Sandy
in the top photo
Looking very "tough"
at 2 ½ years old
On left, Cousins
Debbie & Bonnie
Sandy in middle
On right, Sisters
Judi & Wendy

EACH LIFE IS LIKE A UNIQUE QUILT CREATED BY A PATCHWORK OF MEMORIES STITCHED TOGETHER BY the THREADS OF TIME AND LOVE

Pg. 67

3. In future years we shall recall this PERFECT MOMENT

Pg.

Just Married

4. Snapshots of Time

A HAPPY MEMORY CAPTURED FOREVER

The journey of sharing both laughter and tears
SISTERHOOD
connected together through a lifetime of years

5. WEDDING BELLS

Katie
Holly

What a couple! Holly & Katie Halloween 1984 The girls make a Great bride & Groom giggling and laughing all around the neighbourhood collecting candy treats

Holly

1.

The best Christmas gift of all OUR FAMILY All happily wrapped up in one another

A COUPLE OF CHRISTMAS CUTIES

WHO NEEDS SANTA when you have Nana & Papa

dEaR SaNta LeaVe PreSents Take BRothER Sister

2.

*Dashing*through*the*snow*

Snowmen are the Coolest Guys

SNOWMAN'S PRAYER: Please Freeze AMEN

3.

Christmas the Season of Heart

Inside message reads ...

Hope You're All Wrapped Up In the Spirit of Christmas

5.

HEY Ghoul-Friend YoUR Outfit is SPOOKtacular!

Free Spells Hexes Here

Sugar Bugs

HAPPY HAUNTS TO YOU!

A GHOULISH GROUP OF TREATERS

4.

For Some-Bunny Special WORTH 24 CARROTS

Inside message reads ...

Little HONEY BUNNY

6.

Add expressions or journaling!

Michaels 4th Birthday 1992

To Amanda Love Santa OXOX

Ideas & Supply List
for color sample pages 51 & 52

1. Yakity-Yak
From pg. 36
A perfect page for phone hogs!
Copy page on blue and white. Cut this one out carefully. From blue, cut out the phones staying with-in the dash lines. From white, cut out the center dial staying inside the phone. Color the dots and Miss Chatty in orange and Yakity-Yak in blue felt pens. Cut around white dash lines and mat on to purple. Mount on polk-a-dot print. See a 2nd sample on back cover.

2. Picture Worth a Zillion Words
From pg. 77
For wacky photos.
Out of My Mind and 100% Crazy also from pg. 77. Copy on bright green, yellow and white as shown. Cut out expressions and double mat them with photos on Kangaroo & Joey flower print.

3. Glorious Grins of Greatness
From pg. 81, 82 & 83
Glorious mini page for any grinning performers.
Copy on white and color with felts like sample. Cut out and mat on polka dot paper.

4. Tool Time
From pg. 43
Compliment your handyman with a page or card.
Copy expression and graphic on white and tan. Cut out and mat with wood grain paper from Provo Craft and solid blue. Mount on blue check from Provo Craft.

5. It's a Guy Thing
From pg. 43
Scrapbook the man in your life.
Copy expressions on sand and color them green. Mat with green check and green wave from Keeping Memories Alive, and beige and dark green. Mount on same dark green and green wave paper.

6. King of the Remote
From pg. 42
Calling all couch potatoes!
Copy page on white and gold. Cut out and color with watercolor pencils. Mat photo on stripe paper from Frances Meyer and mount on rust.

7. First Fish
From pg. 85
Great ideas for outdoor adventures.
Copy expressions on cream and beige, color and double mat with brown, mount on tree paper from Provo Craft.

1. Best Christmas
From pg. 17
A page of ideas for family Christmas photos.
Copy expressions and graphics on white. Color with felts and mat with green leaf paper from Keeping Memories Alive and solid red. Mount on red wave check from Keeping Memories Alive.

2. Snowmen Are Cool
From pg. 17
Page idea for snow photos.
Copy designs on white and color. Tear stock to look like snow banks. Mat photos in red and add black hats. Mount everything onto Provo Craft snow flurry paper.

3. Christmas, the Season of Hearts
From pg. 95
A cute Christmas card.
This card was made using the Christmas card template and colored using computer software. Copy page 95 on cream or beige card and color as you wish. Double mat on red and black stock. Note: if you mat this card you will need a larger envelope than the template.

4. For Somebunny Special
From pg. 94
An adorable card for any-bunny!
This card was made using the bunny card design copied on white. Color with felts or pencils. Trace heart shape over a photo for inside. Corners punched with heart punch from Family Treasures. Mount on pastel green and pink and add ribbon.

5. Ghoulish Treaters
From pg. 45
A fun page for Halloween photos.
Copy expressions and graphics on white, yellow and lime green as shown. Cut out and color. Mat with same colors and purple paper. Mount on purple dot paper from Paper Pizazz.

6. Frog & Christmas Stocking Frames
From pg. 97 & 99
All the frames on these pages are perfect for adding other expressions and journaling.
Copy or trace frames on white or colored paper and color to suit your projects.

Extra Extra
Read All About Me!

 100% Cute Kid

 Kids With Class

 Brainiac Kid

 Looking Very Cool For The 1st Day of School

Messy Little Munchkin(s)

Just Kiddin' Around

Hey a little dirt never hurt anyone

Rub-A-Dub-Dub

Look Who's In The Tub!

All Squeaky Clean

Little Streaker

The Kid With a Million Faces

55

LOVE YA KIDDO!

 Cutie Pie(s)

PLAYTIME 101

Our Little Sweetie

The Young & The Restless

 Who Wouldn't LOVE THiS FACE?

 MIRROR MIRROR ON THE WALL WHO'S THE CUTEST KID OF ALL?

In sharing the joys of your **CHILDHOOD** I relived my own

 A Child is a beam of sunlight from GOD

A whole year's gone by and time sure has flown what's really amazing is how you have grown

 ALL tucked in snug as a Bug

Little Sprout

 A LITTLE BOOKWORM

57

MY·PARTNER·MY·BEST·FRIEND
ALL·MY·DREAMS·COME·TRUE
EVERYTHING·I·COULD·WANT
I·FOUND·IN·LOVING·YOU

I would Marry You all over Again and Again

Made For Each other

You'll Be In My Heart Forever

Together We've Got A Little Slice of Heaven

Two Hearts Shall Beat as One

Truly Madly Deeply Crazy For You!

Our Best Gift is Each Other

Tied Together By Our Love

FALLING

Head Over Heels Over You

ONE WORD FREES US OF ALL THE PAIN OF LIFE. THAT WORD IS LOVE

SOPHOCLES

I did not know what I was missing until I found what I had been waiting for—

YOU!

Cuddle Bug(s)

Love & You

Bitten by the Love Bug

I Could Count the ways I Love you Forever

sealed with a K·I·S·S

Love Bugs

walking on cloud nine

Of All The Blessings
I've Possessed
Your Love Is Among
The Very Best~

Some things are simply meant to be,

like finding your soul mate, your heart's destiny.

If I've told you once,
I've told you 1000 times

I LOVE YOU!

Love is a Beautiful Dream

- William Shakespeare 61

Happy Anniversary to a Beautiful Pair
On the Birthday of your Love Affair

Together Forever & Ever Together

True Love Never Goes Out of Style

One Cute Couple

Totally Nuts About You!

1 WAY Ticket on the LOVE TRAIN

I'M COO-KOO over you!

Snuggle Bum

LOVE can make you CRAZY in the most beautiful way

my eyes adore you

We Loved With A Love That Was more Than Love

— Edgar Allan Poe

VIVA AMOUR

You + I from here to ETERNITY

A HAPPY MEMORY Captured Forever

Snapshots of Time

In future years we shall recall this
PERFECT MOMENT

God gave us memories
that we might have Roses
in the December of our lives
~ James M. Barrie

Nothing
is worth more
than this Day
~ Goethe

Cherish
Old Memories
&
Young Hopes

A Lifetime of Sweet Memories

Recall it as often
as you wish
A happy memory
never wears out
- Libby Fideum

TRULY
TOTALLY
TERRIFIC
TIMES
TOGETHER

A moment lasts but a second.
The memory can last f·o·r·e·v·e·r·

Life isn't a matter
of milestones but of
MOMENTS
Rose Kennedy

Legacy Lane

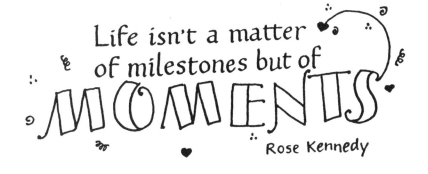

A Day to Remember (Night)
Forever & Ever

GALLERY of GOOD MEMORIES

Taking A Stroll Down Memory Lane

A Glimpse Of The Good 'Ol Times

"That moment," the King went on, "I will never forget!"

"Yes you will though," the Queen said, "Unless you make a memorandum of it."

Lewis Caroll

Each life is like a unique quilt created by a patchwork of memories stitched together by the threads of time and love.

To Live On in the Hearts of those You Leave Behind Is Never to Die

-American Civil War Veteran

Gone But Never Forgotten

Special Memories Fit Together

I Thank My God Upon Every Remembrance Of You

PHILIPPIANS 1:3

READ ALL ABOUT THE GENUINE RELIC!
Over Half A Century Old!

Classified

Senior Antique - Make an Offer!
An Oldie, but a real Goodie!
Real Quality & Style (May need parts)

They don't make 'em like this anymore!

FORGET HEALTH FOOD I Need All The PRESERVATIVES I Can GET!

Truly Madly Deeply Young at Heart

So many Candles So little Cake

Old Croonie formerly known as Stud Muffin

OLD GEEZER

Older THaN DiRT

THESE JOINTS MIGHT BE A LITTLE RUSTY, BUT THERE'S LOTS OF GAS AND PLENTY OF SPARK LEFT

The Kids Are All Grown & Gone, Now It's Time To PARTY!

Now That We Are RETIRED We Can Act Like Goofy Kids

Toasting Golden Moments

Priceless Golden Girlfriends

Age is only a number and mine is unlisted

Sweet Golden Senior Years

FORGET THE WISDOM OF PASSING YEARS I JUST WANT MY SENIORS DISCOUNT!

Forever young in Spirit

The view after 70 is breathtaking

William Maxwell

An oldie but a real goodie

Like A Fine Wine You Just Get Better With Time

FUN FEISTY & 50

OLD? Never. Just Chronologically Gifted

Just when I finally got my Head Together My Body Starts Falling Apart

HELP! I've Caught Scrapbook Fever!

Cause:
Bitten by the Scrapbook Bug

SYMPTOMS:
- Had A Scrap Attack
- Cropped Till I Dropped
- Swollen Scissor Hand
- Kids Call Me Sticker Queen
- Yell Photo-Op In My Sleep
- Victim Of Quadruple Matting Syndrome
- All Food Must Have Edges Scalloped
- Own Enough 12"x 12" Paper to Cover the Town
- Trim Toenails With Decorative Corner Punch

WARNING: SCRAPBOOKING can be HAZARDOUS TO YOUR WEALTH

The Official Scrap-a-Holics Gauge

$

Certifiable Scrap-a-Holic

Obsessed With Scrapbooking

Seek Help Level

Addicted To Scrapbooking

Regular Scrapbooker

Anything Above This Line Is Top Secret To Husbands

Occasional Scrapbooker

To find out if you have scrap-a-holic tendencies Stack All of your scrapbook PAPER Up Against This Certifiably Silly Gauge

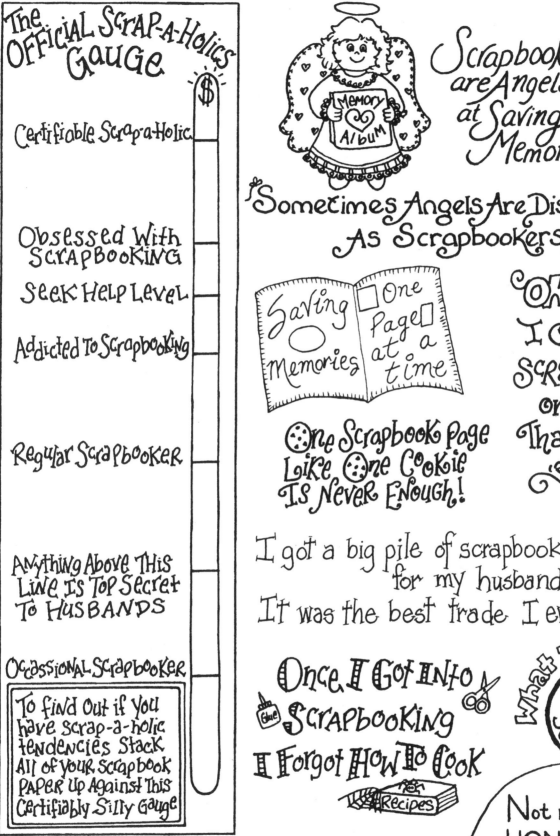

Scrapbookers are Angels at Saving Memories

Memory Album

Sometimes Angels Are Disguised As Scrapbookers.

Saving Memories — One Page at a time

One Scrapbook Page Like One Cookie Is Never Enough!

Oh Sigh, I ONLY Scrapbook on days That end IN "Y"

I got a big pile of scrapbook supplies for my husband
It was the best trade I ever made.

Once I Got Into Scrapbooking I Forgot HOW To Cook

Recipes

What TIME IS IT?

TIME 2 Scrapbook

EEEK! NAKED Pages.

Not now HONEY I'm Scrapbooking

My husband lets me have all the scrapbook supplies I can hide.

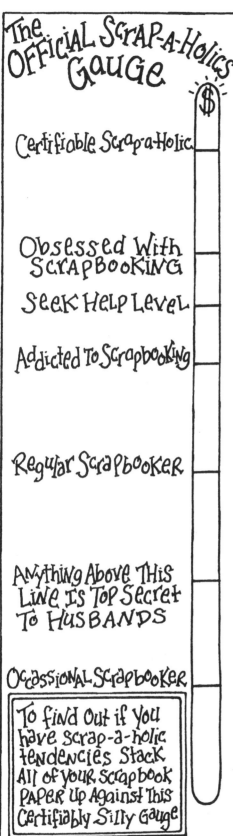

A Spectacularly Splendid
SPRING DAY

We're Having A
HEAT WAVE

Hot Fun
IN THE
Summertime

A Slice of
Summer Memories

IN the
Good
O'l
Summer
Time

Oh Lazy Dazy
Summer Afternoon

A HARVEST of AUTUMN
memories

Awesome
Autumn
Afternoon

Snowflakes
Are
Heaven Sent

Harvest
of
Love

My Heart
Belongs to
Old Man Winter

Our Winter
Wonderland

Ready
To
Hit
The
Slopes

MY MUG SHOTS

THEY CALL ME TROUBLE

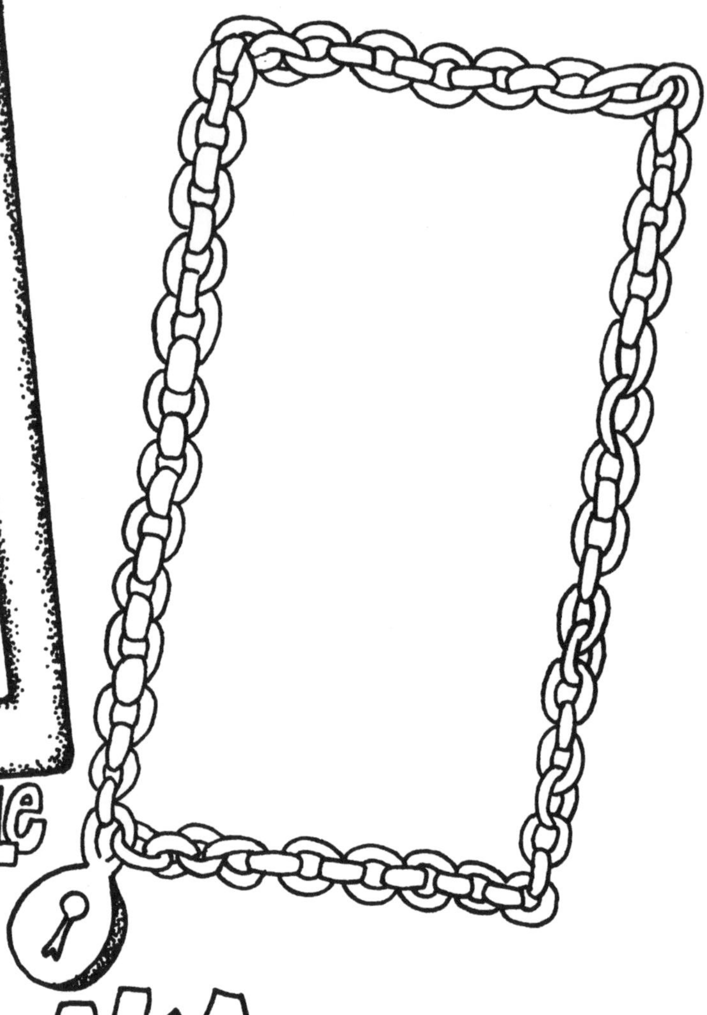

AKA _____

THE MANY FACES OF

_____

A little NONSENSE now and then
is good for even the wisest of men

HAPPY Go DUCKY

BORN 2 PARTY

You can't ever, ever have too much FUN

They call me TROUBLE

Feeling MORE STUFFED Than The TURKEY

Food Fight!

Mischievous is MY Middle Name

The Bottomless Pit

CAUGHT IN THE ACT

JUST CLOWNING AROUND

You don't have to be CRAZY to work here We Train You!

PARTNERS IN CRIME

- Soccer -
It's A Real Kick In The grASS!

FIELD of DREAMS

TEAM SPIRIT

THREE CHEERS for the COACH

Queens of the Field

Racing Rocket

Take me out to the ball game

RUNNING LIKE THE WIND

CERTIFIED SPORTS NUT

BATTY 4 BASEBALL

IN A LEAGUE OF THEIR OWN

Future Olympian

THESE FEET WERE MADE FOR RUNNING

Little SLUGGER

81

ALL STAR ATHLETE

Going The Distance

MVP

Future Hall of Famer

Savoring The Glory

Super Star Swimmer

Swims Like a Fish

The GLORIOUS GRINS OF GREATNESS

THE DEADLY DEFENSE

OUCH!

QUARTERBACK

CUTIE

LION HEARTED PLAYERS

Together Everyone Achieves More

THUNDER FOOT

Our Goal is More Goals

Our Team MASCOT

INCREDIBLE ON ICE

THE PUCK STOPS HERE

Kings ON ICE

THE BEST PART OF OUR TEAM, ARE THE ♡'s OF OUR PLAYERS

Camp-o-rama!

It TAKES REAL GUTS TO CLEAN A FISH

Reel Relaxed At The Lake

IN THE WOODS GOING Squirrelly

NATURE BOY

ATTENTION: All Fish Bite NOW (please!)

CANDID CAMPING MOMENT
GATHERED ROUND THE FIRE GRATEFUL FOR BURNT OFFERINGS

A little slice of heaven.... here on earth

The 1st REEL FISH I ever caught

S'MORE SCARY STORIES

Nature GIRL

RV ADVENTURES

On The Trail To Fun

HOMEWARD BOUND

85

Passport To Paradise

Leaving on a Jet Plane... May Never Come Back Again

THIS SURE BEATS WORK!

I don't need a 2 week vacation, I need the 50 week package please.

ANCHORS AWAY MATES!

'ALL ABOARD!'

CATCHING SOME WAVES

When You look like Your Passport Photo You need a Vacation

BEACH BABES

BeachBumBuddies

SICK OF WORK
NEED A BREAK
TIME TO CATCH
SOME RAYS & BAKE

Certified PSYCHO Wave Runner

Down By The Sea, Down By The Sea

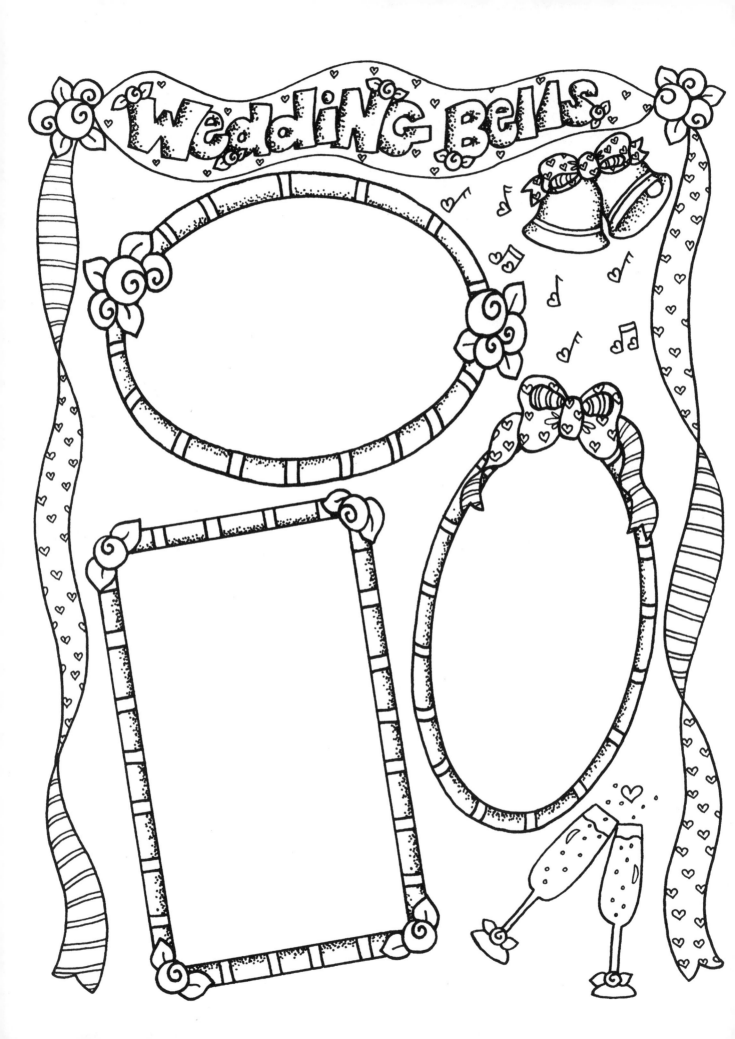

A Celebration of Love

TOGETHER WE STAND
UNITED IN LOVE

Pretty Maids

All in a Row

Look WHO'S FAMILY NOW!

Just Married

From this day forward
My Bride and Joy

Flower Flinging Female Frenzy!

RADIANT Faces of Love

May you grow old on one pillow together
Armenian Proverb

The Guys Galloping For The Garter!

may I have this dance for the rest of my life?

Honeymoon Sweeties

Get Me To The Church On Time!

89

Saving Memories One Page At A Time

Use This Page
to Add Your Own
Favorite Expressions

ringing in the

NEW YEAR

Joy of Christmas

Valentines ♥♥ Loving You

LOOK WHOS HAVING A
BIRTHDAY

Summertime Fun

Gathered together with
Thankful Hearts

BIRTHDAYS Area Piece of Cake!

Happy Birthday

Made just for you by

Crafty Secrets Publications

_____

Hip·Hip Hooray

It's Your

Birthday

Today!

Please Hop Over To:

_____

At: _____

On: _____

For A Toadly Fun Time!

Your invited to a

BIG
Birthday
Bash

Hop on Over
To my Pad
For A Toadly
Fun Party!

Crafty Secrets Publications

This card made just for you by

_____

Little Know How Emma

From Your

WORTH 24 CARROTS

Some-Bunny

Special

For

Made just for you by _____

_____

Made just for you by

Christmas the Season of Heart~

Hope You're All
Wrapped Up In
the Spirit of Christmas

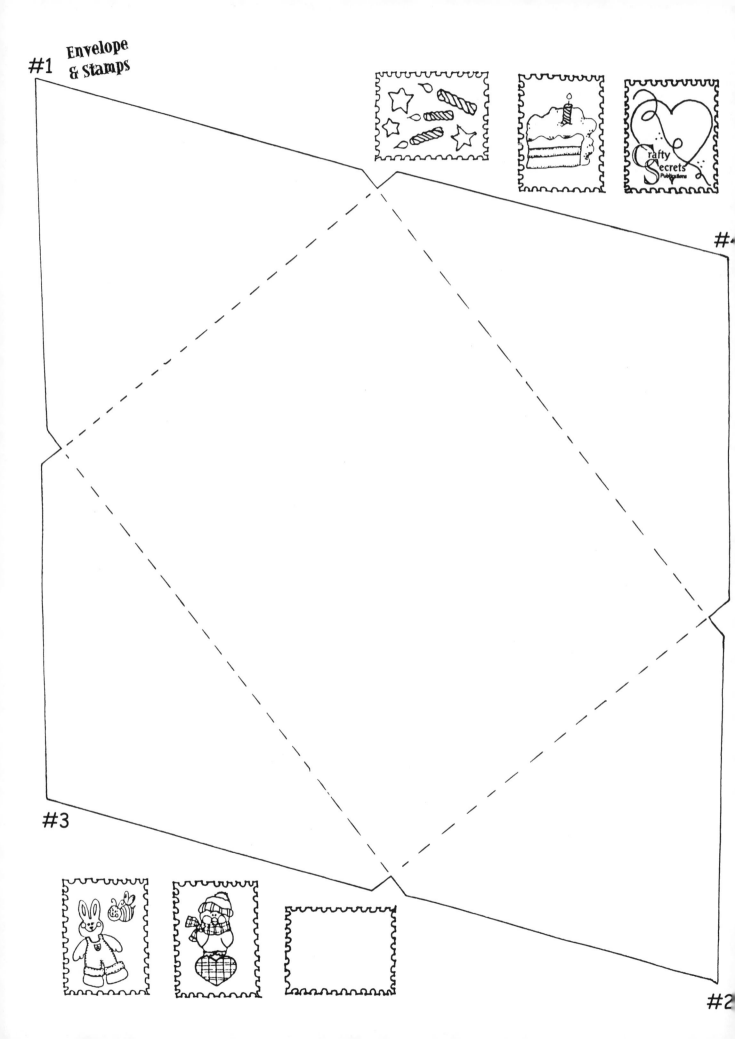

Envelope
& Stamps

#1

#3

#2

Some of My Favorite Supplies and Resources

Paper and Scrapbook Supplies

DMD Industries
(Paper Reflections)
www.dmdind.com

Frances Meyer Inc
www.francesmeyer.com

Kangaroo and Joey Inc
(480) 460-4841
aschneid@gateway.net

Keeping Memories Alive
(800) 419-4949
www.scrapbooks.com

Paper Adventures
(800) 727-0699
www.paperadventures.com

Paper Pizazz
(Hot Off the Press)
(503) 266-9102
www.paperpizazz.com

Provo Craft
(801) 794-9000
www.provocraft.com

Please Note:
I haven't specified any specific suppliers for un-patterned paper or card stock, as it is available from so many sources. Check your favorite retailer for colors.

Watch for our NEW Heartwarming Expressions STICKERS in Jan. 2002!

Scrapbook Supplies

Craft-T-Products
(Decorating Chalks)
(507) 235-3996

EK Success
(Zig Memory System Products)
www.eksuccess.com

Family Treasures
(661) 294-1330
www.familytreasures.com

Inspire Graphics
(801) 235-9393
www.letteringdelights.com

Sakura of America
www.gellyroll.com

Staedtler
(818) 882-6000
www.staedtler-usa.com

Therm O Web
Wholesale only
www.thermoweb.com

For Inspiration and Knowledge

Creating Keepsakes
(801) 984-2070
www.creatingkeepsakes.com

Ivy Cottage Creations
(888) 303-1375
ivycottagecreations.com

Memory Makers
(303) 452-1968
www.memorymakers
magazine.com

PC Create It Magazine
(Computer & photo crafts for PC & Mac)
(864) 286-0540
www.pccreateit.com

PaperKuts Magazine
(801) 426-4546
www.papercuts.com

**Scrapbooks Etc.
Magazine**
(Better Homes and Gardens)
www.bhg.com

**Somerset Studios
Magazine**
(510) 553-9800
www.somersetstudios.com

My only regret . . .

I forgot to take photos of us working on the samples so I could make a scrapbook page of us scrap-a-holics!

WARNING
I have PMS & Scissors
Positively Maniac Scrapbooker
Syndrome

Rx Relief
♡ Cozy Jammies
♡ ½ Pint Ice Cream
♡ Favorite Scrapbook Magazine
~Dr. Crop-a-Lot